LILLY SINGH

The Ultimate Unofficial

SUPERWOMAN GUIDE

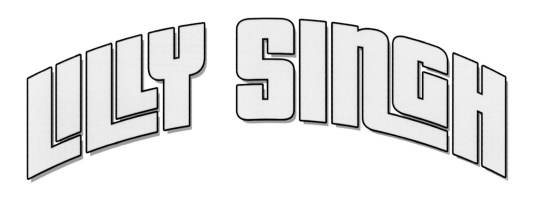

LILY SINGH

The Ultimate Unofficial
SUPERWOMAN GUIDE

Jo Berry

This edition first published in Great Britain in 2016 by Orion
an imprint of the Orion Publishing Group Ltd
Carmelite House
50 Victoria Embankment
London EC4Y 0DZ
An Hachette UK Company

1 3 5 7 9 10 8 6 4 2

A CIP catalogue record for this book is available from the British Library.

ISBN: 978 1 4091 6860 7

Designed by www.us-now.com

Printed in Italy

The Orion Publishing Group's policy is to use papers that are natural, renewable and
recyclable and made from wood grown in sustainable forests. The logging and manufacturing
processes are expected to conform to the environmental regulations of the country of origin.

Every effort has been made to fulfil requirements with regard to
reproducing copyright material. The author and publisher will be
glad to rectify any omissions at the earliest opportunity.

PICTURE CREDITS:
IStock: AdiniMalibuBarbie: p30/31; Alex Belomlinsky: p52; Alphotographic: p37;
AnnaKandelaki: p51; Calvindexter: p53; Charles Schug: p25; Croisy: p15; Daniel Rodríguez
Quintana: p44; Fighter_Francevna: p34; GlobalP: p49; Ikopylov: p60; Inides: p17; Isaac
Marzioli: p25; Jennifer Borton: p52; Lauri Patterson: p14/15; Ly86: p13; Manuta: p36;
Meral Yildirim: p25; Murdock48: p48; Rebius: p58; Sonya_illustration: p49; Surangaw: p4;
Getty: p9, p16, p12, p23, p26.7, p28/29, p38 p42/43, p47, p63; PA Images: p2, p6/7,
p.56/57, p.58/59; Rexfeatures: p22, p.28, p31.

www.orionbooks.co.uk

CONTENTS

QUICK FACT

Name: Lilly Singh

Date of birth: 26 September 1988

Height: 5ft 5in

Home town: Lilly grew up in Scarborough, Ontario, in Canada, but now lives in Los Angeles

Family: Lilly's parents are originally from Punjab, India. She has an older sister named Tina

School: She has a degree in psychology from York University in Canada

Favourite food: Popcorn – she asks for it at every gig she performs at

Favourite movie: *Willy Wonka and the Chocolate Factory* (the 1971 movie with Gene Wilder, not *Charlie and the Chocolate Factory* (2005) with Johnny Depp)

Eye colour: Dark brown, but in the sun Lilly says people have told her they look hazel

DOWNLOAD

Hair colour: Black – and it is very long, past her waist!

Favourite places to visit: Mumbai in India and Singapore

Phobias: Spiders and clowns

Favourite book: *Confessions of a Shopaholic* by Sophie Kinsella

Favourite musician: Bob Marley

Favourite TV show: *Game of Thrones*

Girl crush: Selena Gomez

Boy crush: Dwayne 'The Rock' Johnson

Lilly's Superstar Journey

Lilly Singh, the YouTube star known as Superwoman, was born on 26 September 1988 in Scarborough, Ontario, Canada, which Lilly herself describes as a pretty rough neighbourhood. But she loved growing up there, with her mum, dad and sister Tina and, despite being something of a tomboy, was a Girl Guide during her school years, selling cookies to her neighbours to raise money.

Lilly was also pretty smart – no surprise there! – and she was valedictorian (top of the leavers' class) at her elementary (primary) school. When she wasn't singing along to her favourite bands, the Backstreet Boys and the Spice Girls, she was dreaming of meeting her idol, The Rock, never imagining her dream would one day come true.

It was while Lilly was growing up that she bought a chunky silver ring with the Superman 'S' symbol on it, that she still wears today. She explains that thinking of herself as Superwoman got her through a lot of tough times growing up.

Lilly always dreamed she would become a superstar rapper or an actress when she was older, and knew that sitting behind a desk would not be a career move for her, but even so she decided to go to university to study psychology rather than pursue her celebrity dreams. It was during her third year at uni that Lilly began to suffer from depression, and had problems with her college friends. It became so hard for Lilly that she could barely make it out of bed in the morning, and she lost a lot of friends who didn't understand what she was going through.

Her depression lasted for around a year, and Lilly's not sure what happened to change her feelings, but one day she decided she just couldn't carry on as she had been. Scary as it was, she worked really hard to be happy, positive and strong, and after taking time to recover slowly, she started to think about what lay ahead for her.

Lilly had posted a few YouTube videos online and decided it was something she loved doing and wanted to focus on. She wanted to create videos that would make people's days better – make them laugh, make them think and make them smile. She started her Superwoman channel in 2010 and posted videos that included impersonations of her parents, rants about things in her life and vlogs where she talked about her own fears and hopes. She also told fans about her happy place, Unicorn Island, and shared her advice on how to be strong and positive.

Since her channel launched, Lilly has gone from a few subscribers to over eight million. She's released songs, including '#LEH' and '#IVIVI' with her friend Humble The Poet, and in 2014 she played herself in two movies, *Gulaab Gang* and *Dr Cabbie,* where she met her friend Kunal Nayyar (best known as Raj in *The Big Bang Theory*).

Read on for more about the amazing Lilly Singh . . .

Lilly has already won two major awards for her Superwoman YouTube channel – The MTV Fandom Awards' Social Superstar of the Year 2015 and the Streamy First Person award 2015 – congratulations Lilly!

FANDOM
‼ ♡ AWARDS ♡ ‼

LILLY'S CATCHPHRASES

If you like it, subscribe!

TALK LIKE A BADASS!

Part of the fun of watching Lilly's videos is her quick-fire, funny delivery and her cute catchphrases like these:

If you don't know me well, now you do!

One love, Superwoman – that is a wrap – and zoop!

What up, everyone!

Unicorn Island

Unicorn Island is basically Lilly's happy place, a place that she has shared with all her fans. And she has millions of fans who understand all the things Lilly has gone through, from lacking confidence to being scared about what comes next, and her positivity has inspired them. If Lilly can pull herself up, be strong and carry on, we can all do it!

As Lilly herself has explained: 'Unicorn Island is that state I reach when I decide "Everything's gonna be OK", and I'm happy because life is great.'

So how can we all reach our own Unicorn Island? Here is some advice Lilly has given to her fans:

- You do not need anyone to be happy besides yourself.
- Happiness is the only thing worth fighting for in life.
- You can do whatever you want to do in life. Just believe.
- If you find a job or career you like, work really hard at it and you'll see the rewards.
- Always stay true to who you are.
- You can be your own superhero. Just be brave!
- When things get you down, remember – life is beautiful and you are awesome!
- Don't get caught up in all the things that are going wrong. Think of the things that are all right, and remember your happy place.
- Don't surround yourself with negative people as they'll only bring you down.

REMEMBER: Unicorn Island is the place where there is no wrong, no right, no one is arguing what is real and what is not. It's the place that makes you happy.

Lilly's Beauty Inspiration:

The many looks of Lilly Singh and how to achieve them

Lilly has actually made fun of make-up tutorials – check out her 'Inner Beauty Make–up Tutorial', it's hilarious (www.youtube.com/watch?v=1HZuFmX0p5g) – and she is happy to appear in her videos without anything on her face at all. But when Lilly does wear make-up, she knows exactly what suits her, whether she is going for a natural or a glamorous look. Here are some helpful tips so you can be make-up confident too:

Choosing Your Make–up

First of all, don't assume that you have to spend a lot of money on make-up. Just because a brand is expensive, it doesn't mean that it is any better than a cheaper one! If you find it difficult to decide which foundation shade or lipstick colour suits you, take a friend along for a second opinion. Out shopping alone? Many high–street brands now do colour-matching, where an assistant matches foundation and lipstick to your skin tone so you're confident you've chosen the right shades.

You also don't need a suitcase full of make-up, either. The only essentials you need in your make-up bag are:

- Concealer
- Primer
- Liquid or powder foundation or CC cream (depending on how much coverage you want)
- Bronzer or blusher
- Eyeshadow and/or eyeliner
- Mascara
- Lipstick or lip gloss
- Make-up brushes

Get the Look: Natural

1. Make sure your skin is clean, then apply a moisturiser that suits your skin type. If your skin is dry, pay special attention to the drier areas. If your skin tends to be greasy, avoid oil-based moisturisers. Allow the moisturiser to dry for a minute.

2. Apply primer to your skin. Primer has become a must-have product, as there are primers that deal with skin problems such as visible pores or uneven skin tone, and also because they provide a base that helps your make-up last longer. You only need a little, so apply sparingly. Some primers are quite wet, so make sure the primer has dried before you continue.

3. Begin by applying concealer on any blemishes or areas where your skin is red, to even out your skin colour. Make sure the concealer is the same shade or one shade lighter than your skin tone – darker or paler than that and it will show! You can also use it on dark under-eye circles, too. Blend the concealer in using a brush or your fingers.

4. Apply foundation to your face as evenly as possible, making sure you blend it in to your neck, too. Hopefully you've chosen a shade close to your own skin tone so it will blend in easily. You can use a make-up sponge, a make-up brush or your fingers to apply a liquid foundation. If you are using a powder, use the buff or sponge provided or a large foundation brush to apply the powder lightly and evenly (you don't want it to look cakey). If you find liquid and powder foundations too heavy, look at the more lightweight BB and CC creams that give your skin a fresh finish.

5. Using a large brush, take a small amount of bronzer and brush it onto your cheekbones. You can also use the powder to lightly highlight your forehead if you wish.

6. For a natural eye, first shade your eyebrows to lightly fill them in. You can use an eyebrow pencil or a tiny bit of shadow that matches your eyebrow hair colour. If you're happy with how full your eyebrows are, simply use a toothbrush to brush them in one direction so they look tidy, or use clear mascara.

7. Choose a natural or nude powder shade on your eyelids, applied with an applicator or small brush. Then apply a slightly darker shade of brown to the crease above your eyelids and blend in.

8. If you want to wear eyeliner, use dark brown or black and make a fine line along your lashline – don't go too dramatic for daytime!

9. Apply mascara, doing your lower lashes first, followed by the upper lashes – that way, you are less likely to smudge.

10. For lips, choose a nude or natural shade to keep the look simple for daytime, or go for a nude or clear gloss on your lips.

Lilly's Hairstyles

We haven't all got hair down to our waists like Lilly, but luckily her hairstyles work on different lengths of hair, so we can all try out her great looks. Here are some tips on how to get Lilly-fabulous hair for yourself:

Straight and Sleek

Lilly often wears her hair straight, and it looks beautifully shiny. To achieve the same look, you need to take care of your hair, having regular trims to keep the ends neat. You also need to use a shampoo and conditioner that work well for your type of hair, be it fine, tangled, dry, greasy or normal. Then, to get the straight and sleek look:

1. Once you have washed your hair, gently towel-dry it (HANDY TIP: If your hair is prone to breakage or is frizzy, use an old t-shirt to dry your hair rather than a towel as it is gentler on your hair).

2. Apply a serum to your hair, such as one to protect from heat damage.

3. Using a round brush, gently blow-dry your hair in sections, using the brush to give body and straighten your hair.

4. If your hair is short or fine, this may do the trick. But if you have thicker, longer hair, use ceramic tongs to straighten your hair in sections (the easiest way is to pin back your hair with clips and straighten one area at a time).

5. If you have some, spray your hair with shine finishing spray, and you're done! (Or, to be even more like Lilly, top it off with a baseball cap!)

17

Full and Wavy

For the launch of her movie *A Trip to Unicorn Island,* Lilly wore her hair to the side and falling over one shoulder in waves. To achieve this look, wash and condition your hair and then:

1. Towel-dry as before, then add a serum to prevent styling damage and a small amount of styling mousse or gel for hold.

2. Rough-dry your hair to give it body. Just run your hands through your hair while you are drying it with a hairdryer.

3. Divide your hair into sections with clips (e.g. the fringe, if you have one, each side, a few sections at the back . . .). Make sure you give yourself a side parting and decide which way you want your hair to fall.

4. You want your hair to go in one direction, towards the shoulder it will be falling over (for example, if you have given yourself a parting on the left, you want your hair to fall towards the right). Starting at the parting side, take small vertical sections of hair and curl them with tongs so that you create a long, vertical wave each time. Work in one direction, curling hair the same way each time so that the curls are all going towards the shoulder on the opposite side to your parting.

5. Once you have curled your whole head into what may look like ringlets (don't panic!), let your hair cool down. And don't forget to turn off the curling tongs! (If you haven't got tongs, heated rollers will work just as well. Or, if you just have foam rollers, dry your hair until it is not quite dry, place it in the rollers and finish drying with a hairdryer. Leave them in while your hair cools and then carefully take them out.)

6. Once your hair is completely cool, take a vented hairbrush and gently brush your hair, turning the curls into waves. Make sure you brush in the direction you want your hair to go. Add a tiny drop of shine serum to hold the waves and add gloss to your look.

7. If your hair is short, you can always hide a few hair grips on the parting side to hold your style, so it is fuller on one side than the other.

Dramatic Up-Do

For the Streamy Awards, Lilly wore her long hair in a bun on the top of her head. It's actually an easier look to achieve than you'd think, and here's how:

1. Wash and dry your hair as for the Straight and Sleek style, on page 17.

2. Using a brush, scrape your hair back from your face and tie it into a ponytail using a stretchy hair band. Don't just use a plain elastic band, as it snags your hair – make sure it is one for hair use. Decide how high you want your ponytail as the base is where the bun will be. Lilly wore hers quite high on her head but if your hair is short, it looks just as cool at the back of your head.

3. Take a handful of hairgrips/bobby pins and start twisting your ponytail around on itself until you have a bun shape.

4. Tuck the ends of your ponytail into the bun so they are hidden, and place hairgrips there and around the bun to secure it.

5. If you have mid-length or short hair, you may find it easier to use a doughnut – one of those foam rings you can buy in most chemists and beauty stores. Make the ponytail as above, then pull the doughnut over it and place it at the base of the ponytail. Now simply tuck your hair around the doughnut until you can't see the foam ring any more, and secure with hairpins.

Smoothie Challenge!

Like many YouTubers, Lilly is up for a challenge – especially if it's of the smoothie variety! Her 'Smoothie Challenge' has been watched by over four million people, and you can have a go at home, too.

You'll need:

- electric blender/juicer or electric whisk and a bowl
- 10 foods if two people playing (see below for examples) – you'll need more choices for more players
- a drinking glass for each person
- kitchen towel and a waste bin to hand, just in case!
- a glass of water for each player, as you may need to rinse your mouth out!

1. Collect together five 'good' items, things that go well in smoothies like Oreo cookies and bananas, and five 'bad' items like ketchup and curry sauce, and number each item from 1 to 10.

2. Put 10 numbered pieces of paper in a hat and take turns picking a number. Each one corresponds to one of the foods, so when you choose a number, that food has to go in your smoothie!

3. Once you have five foods in your glass, you have to blend them together and then take a sip. It's easiest if you can blend them in an electric blender (don't forget to put the lid on) and then pour the mixture into a glass.

4. The challenge is to see who is brave enough to give their smoothie a try!

Some suggestions for foods you can use:

Good

Strawberries

Blueberries

Bananas

Honey

Yogurt

Oreo cookies
(better than regular cookies,
as they are softer!)

Chocolate sauce

Whipped cream

Chocolate chips

Chocolate milk

Bad

Vegemite/Marmite

Ketchup

Mustard

Pickles

Salad dressing

Curry sauce

BBQ sauce

Salt and pepper

Dried herbs

Sour cream

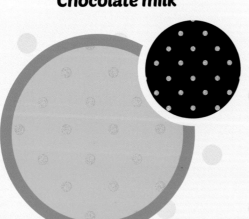

The Lilly Look

Rather than obsessively follow fashion, Lilly has the right attitude – she chooses clothes she loves and feels comfortable in, and because she has confidence in her own style she always looks good. Like Lilly, the best thing you can do is discover what suits you and what you are happy in, whether it's heels and a strappy dress for an evening out, or jeans and sneakers for a casual day in. Here are some of Lilly's favourite looks to give you some ideas:

Red Carpet

Since gaining zillions of fans on YouTube, Lilly has been invited to a few red carpet events, including the premiere of her own movie, *A Trip to Unicorn Island*. She often wears red or black for an evening occasion, going for either a jumpsuit or a knee-length dress teamed with heels. If you're very tall, you may not find jumpsuits that fit properly (remember, most clothes are styled for an 'average' height of just 5ft 6in!) as they are often too short in the body as well as the legs, but you can achieve the same look with a matching pair of trousers and a fitted top or blazer. Stores like Zara and Topshop have a lot of these. If you're more of a dress fan, either go for a little black dress, as Lilly sometimes has (you can add some fun with brightly coloured shoes and a bag), or choose a bright primary colour that suits you to really stand out. Lilly's favourite colour is red, and it is a colour that looks great on most people. If that's too bold for you, try a bright blue (this colour looks especially good on blondes and redheads) or sun yellow (great for darker skin tones – beware if you are pale, as it can wash you out).

TOP TIP! If you are going for a bright dress or jumpsuit, keep your accessories simple – gold or silver-coloured jewellery and either nude, black or metallic shoes and bag. Any more colour and you'll look like you got style tips from a bag of M&Ms!

The Lilly Look...

Graphic Tees and Kicks

For a lot of her YouTube videos, Lilly appears in her favourite combination of jeans, a graphic t-shirt and a pair of brightly coloured trainers. Her graphic tees have featured the 'S' Superman/Supergirl logo, her own Unicorn Island graphic and various fun slogans, and it's easy to recreate the look yourself. Just choose a t-shirt with a logo, band art or comic book character that you like – there are lots to choose from in stores like Topshop, Primark and Urban Outfitters – and wear it with your favourite jeans. Top the look off with sunglasses and sneakers, and you're ready to go.

TOP TIP! If you can't afford a new graphic t-shirt, grab an old plain tee from your wardrobe and write or stencil on your own quote or graphic (you can buy laundry pens that don't wash out at stationery or craft stores). Just remember to keep it simple (. . . and clean! No rude slogans!).

Going Casual

Lilly lives in LA now, a place where most people dress casually, partly due to the hot weather! While her graphic tees and kicks look works well (see above), Lilly sometimes changes her style by adding a check shirt over a t-shirt and black jeans, or wearing a sports-style t-shirt dress. A fan of bright colours, she's also been known to smarten up her look with a bright yellow blazer. The basic rule is, if it's comfortable, it's cool! Find your own style by choosing a type of blouse or shirt you really like and wearing it over a t-shirt, along with black jeans or leggings. Polo-shirt dresses, shirt dresses and sports t-shirt dresses are all on trend right now, so if you'd rather ditch the jeans, you'll find plenty of these in stores like Zara, H&M and online at ASOS.com.

TOP TIP! Keep your look casual with sneakers for the day – you can dress up a t-shirt dress with heels for the evening, giving you two looks for the price of one!

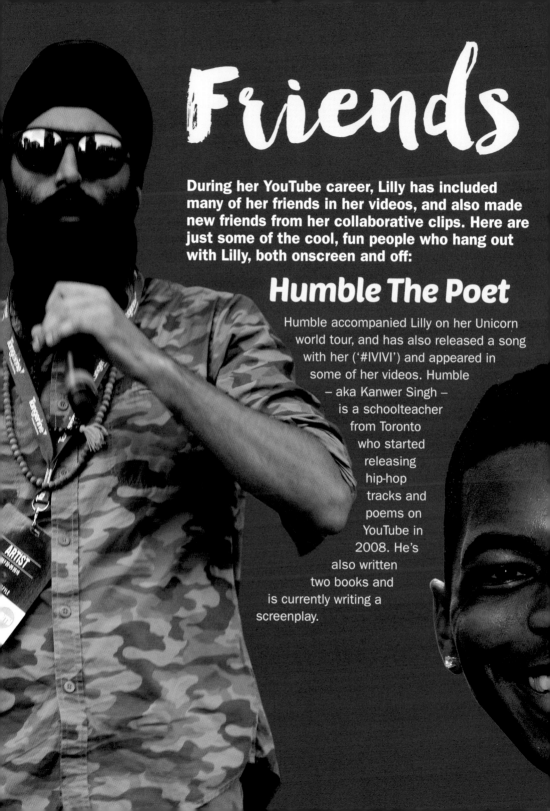

Friends

During her YouTube career, Lilly has included many of her friends in her videos, and also made new friends from her collaborative clips. Here are just some of the cool, fun people who hang out with Lilly, both onscreen and off:

Humble The Poet

Humble accompanied Lilly on her Unicorn world tour, and has also released a song with her ('#IVIVI') and appeared in some of her videos. Humble – aka Kanwer Singh – is a schoolteacher from Toronto who started releasing hip-hop tracks and poems on YouTube in 2008. He's also written two books and is currently writing a screenplay.

& Collabs

Grace Helbig

Grace and Lilly have done a few videos together, including 'The 5 Stages to Becoming a Fangirl' and 'The Girl Code', and have become good friends. Grace is an American comedian, actress and YouTuber from New Jersey who, like Lilly, now lives in LA. As well as posting comedy videos on the channel, she makes regular appearances on TV chat shows and has written two books.

Kingsley

Lilly tried the jellybean challenge with her pal Kingsley, and he's in her 'Expectations Vs Reality: Friends' clip, too. He's got his own YouTube channel, of course, where he talks about pop culture, and his own website, kingofculture.com.

Ryan Higa

Also known by his YouTube name Nigahiga, Ryan was born in Hawaii and now lives in Las Vegas. He started his YouTube career lip-synching to songs back in 2006, and now has over 16 million subscribers who love his comedy videos. Ryan made the 'Rules of Racism' video with Lilly.

Miranda Sings

Along with Grace Helbig and Mamrie Hart, Miranda has contributed to a few of Lilly's videos. She's actually the creation of American comedian/actress Colleen Evans, and is meant to be a quirky character who sings and dances badly and gives the worst tutorials on YouTube that you've ever seen!

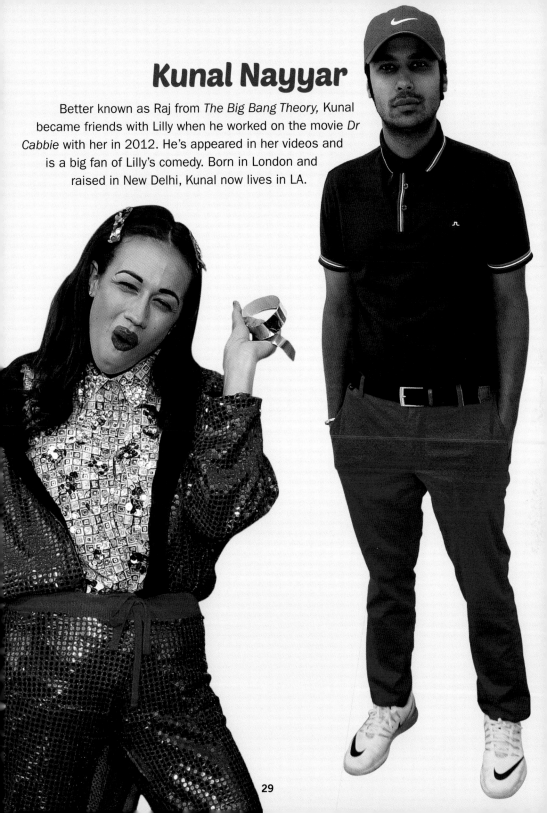

Kunal Nayyar

Better known as Raj from *The Big Bang Theory,* Kunal became friends with Lilly when he worked on the movie *Dr Cabbie* with her in 2012. He's appeared in her videos and is a big fan of Lilly's comedy. Born in London and raised in New Delhi, Kunal now lives in LA.

On Tour
with Lilly
We're off to
UNICORN ISLAND

After doing some YouTube events where she shared the stage with her fellow vloggers, Lilly realised she wanted to have her own show, where she could talk directly to her fans. So she chatted to her manager Sarah about the possibility of going on tour, and her idea became . . . A Trip to Unicorn Island!

Lilly described her tour idea as 'Katy Perry meets Miley Cyrus meets Willy Wonka and Alice in Wonderland.' She had an idea of what her stage would look like, even making a model featuring mega cupcakes and ice cream cones to explain it, as it would represent her own happy place, Unicorn Island. The concert itself would be a mix of her dancing (with backup dancers), singing, rapping, talking and doing comedy. It was quite an undertaking that involved lots of planning, lots of people and lots of money, too!

Rehearsals took place in Lilly's home city of Toronto, with choreographer Chase teaching eight dancers and Lilly, and one of her first tasks was to jump over one of her fellow dancers! After one attempt – in which Lilly thought she had hit the dancer as she jumped (she hadn't) – Lilly wisely practised in a corner, jumping over a suitcase instead!

Up until the very last minute, Lilly and her team were getting things ready for the tour, including visas and passports for the dancers and crew, costumes and animation for the big screen behind her on the stage. It was all incredibly hard work, but on 19 May 2015 Lilly took to the stage in Mumbai for the first night of her tour!

Wearing a blue sequined pilot jacket, she took her fans on a trip to Unicorn Island, singing, dancing and talking about being happy, and filling the room with happiness, too!

There were some setbacks – one dancer damaged her nose during a routine; Lilly and some of her dancers were ill; one venue in Australia was a lot smaller than they expected and they were all squashed on the stage – but the show was a huge success, and people all over the world got to become a part of Team Super.

Here is where Lilly visited on her

Vancouver, Canada

Manchester, England

Montreal, Canada

Toronto, Canada

Seattle, USA

Chicago, USA

Washington DC, USA

San Francisco, USA

Boston, USA

Kansas City, USA

Anaheim, California, USA

Hartford, USA

Miami, USA

Port of Spain, Trinidad and Tobago

World Tour:

Birmingham, England

London, England

Dubai, United Arab Emirates

Mumbai, India   Hong Kong

Bangalore, India

Singapore

Brisbane, Australia

Sydney, Australia

Perth, Australia

Melbourne, Australia

Adelaide, Australia

The True or False Challenge

Think you know everything there is to know about Lilly? Check out the statements below about her life, and decide which are true and which are false! Answers on p. 64 . . .

1. Lilly is double-jointed in her hands.

2. She's allergic to peanut butter.

3. She admits she swears a lot.

4. Lilly doesn't drink tea or coffee and has never tried either.

5. Her favourite Spice Girl was Posh Spice.

6. When she was little, she was terrified of rollercoasters but now she loves them.

7. She's a vegetarian who also doesn't eat eggs . . . unless they are in pancakes or a cake!

8. Lilly was a very girly girl growing up, always wearing pink.

9. She's been frightened of clowns since she saw the movie of Stephen King's *It* as a child.

10. When she was growing up, Lilly wanted to be an actress or a rapper.

11. Her favourite TV show as a kid was *The Care Bears.*

12. If she could marry a superhero, it would be Superman.

13. The article of clothing Lilly hates the most is culottes.

14. 7,000 people watched Lilly's first YouTube video.

15. Lilly has been described as the 'Punjabi Tina Fey'.

16. When she travels, Lilly always takes 10 different hats with her.

17. When she hit 1,000 subscribers, she made a Justin Bieber parody video called 'Never Say Never' to celebrate.

18. Lilly had a small part in the movie *Dr Cabbie,* a horror movie made in Canada.

19. One of Lilly's good friends is Johnny Galecki, who plays Leonard in *The Big Bang Theory.*

20. The one movie Lilly can't watch is *The Lion King* because it upsets her so much.

At Lilly's Place

Lilly moved to her first apartment in December 2015, and what a place it is! Her Los Angeles home has two bedrooms, a walk-in closet and lots of big windows, plus, most importantly, a whole floor upstairs that she uses to film her videos.

On the main level, beautiful wood floors lead to a bedroom with a balcony, a second bedroom with a huge closet and bathroom and a big living area that has enough space for sofas, a dining table and chairs. Huge windows all around give Lilly an amazing view of the city. In this area there is also an open-plan kitchen with a big American fridge freezer, of course, and another balcony for soaking up the sun, plus metal stairs that lead to the gallery room that Lilly uses as her office.

We're so jealous! Of course, we can't all have a sunny California apartment, but you can recreate a lot of the looks that Lilly has in her home in your own room.

Light and Bright

Like Lilly, take advantage of any sunlight that comes into your room by painting most of the walls white. Lilly had one wall in her living area painted a stunning ocean blue colour, perfect for her LA surroundings, but a light, pretty blue works well in most rooms to add a sunshine feel. If your room is quite cold, go for a sunny yellow to add some warmth to one wall.

Furniture

Lilly's a big fan of IKEA, and their simple, clean furniture is perfect for a modern room. If you are just updating your room and don't need new furniture, brighten up what you have with some white paint – a wooden bedside table or cabinet will look fresh and new without too much effort. Just follow these simple steps:

1. Empty out the wooden item you are going to paint and give it a good clean. And make sure you have permission to paint it!

2. Lay an old sheet down on the floor so you don't make a mess and place the table/cabinet on it.

With some sandpaper, sand down the surfaces you want to paint (if you paint straight onto varnished wood it doesn't coat properly and looks terrible!).

3. Carefully paint the piece of furniture with a coat of undercoat/primer in white. This is a base coat, so make sure it is nice and even. Allow the paint to dry completely.

4. Paint the cabinet or table with your choice of white paint. For a shiny finish, choose a gloss paint for wood, or for a matt finish, choose an eggshell paint.

5. Let the paint dry. You will probably need at least two coats of paint to get the clean, fresh look you want. Make sure you allow the paint to dry between each coat (it's not fun painting on top of sticky paint that hasn't dried!), and let your finished painted furniture dry for at least a day and a night before you use it.

Soft Furnishings

When Lilly moved into her apartment it was completely bare apart from one blue wall and a few bits of white furniture! Since then, she has added some bright touches including a yellow chair and a bright yellow clock, some fantastic comic book posters by French artist Gregoire Guillemin (www.greg-guillemin.com), a piece of Superwoman art by Jason Ratliff (www.jason-ratliff.com) and wall stickers of inspirational quotes. Meanwhile, in her bathroom she has added some red accessories and a brightly patterned shower curtain.

To get Lilly's look, all you need to do is choose a bright primary colour (red, blue or yellow) and use it to add some extra interest to your white room. Most supermarkets and home stores sell cheap, fun little accessories in these colours – add a yellow clock like Lilly's, some red cups or mugs, or a blue rug or cushions to your room.

For the walls, have a look in card shops for any artwork you like – a postcard or greetings card put in a clip frame will add some fun to the room without you having to spend very much money. Or create your own art! Frame your own photo or drawing, or cut out a favourite illustration from a comic book and put that on your wall. Then sit back and enjoy!

SUPER WORDSEARCH

We've picked out some words associated with Lilly's life and hidden them in this wordsearch for you to find. See how quickly you can spot them, and test your friends, too! Words are hidden vertically, horizontally, diagonally and backwards as well as forwards! Happy hunting . . .

Y	A	D	W	A	Y	N	E	J	O	H	N	S	O	N
Z	O	H	P	M	G	B	R	I	S	E	A	D	F	C
D	Q	U	R	L	H	T	A	M	H	J	U	N	P	S
I	M	A	T	E	A	M	S	U	P	E	R	A	E	H
F	O	K	B	U	E	A	M	E	G	H	M	L	R	O
H	S	W	D	D	B	B	A	I	T	E	E	S	C	M
I	R	I	T	G	L	E	O	B	I	G	A	I	B	G
P	E	V	F	E	V	T	H	B	N	W	P	N	S	P
S	U	P	E	R	W	O	M	A	N	D	M	R	A	I
H	W	U	H	O	I	R	S	C	A	O	K	O	L	L
A	S	J	G	P	L	O	C	R	P	T	A	C	V	F
K	P	E	X	A	L	N	I	D	B	J	T	I	N	A
E	W	S	L	F	F	T	H	R	O	M	S	N	U	E
R	A	T	T	C	U	O	W	B	C	U	V	U	S	D
B	L	O	M	E	I	G	S	Y	M	A	E	R	T	S

SUPERWOMAN	LOS ANGELES	DR CABBIE
TORONTO	UNICORN ISLAND	TEAM SUPER
YOUTUBE	HIPSHAKER	TINA
STREAMYS	DWAYNE JOHNSON	HUMBLE

Unicorn Inspo!

Lilly has shared her own life with her fans, both the ups and the downs, and she has some great motivational advice and inspiring words to share, often with a good dose of humour thrown in. Here are just some of her words of wisdom that can inspire and help us all:

- Don't think that your brain controls you – you control your brain! So when you are scared, upset or angry, don't use your feelings as an excuse not to do things. Tell your brain to be brave!

- Remember this when you get hurt – negatives are not forever. Everything you thought you couldn't overcome, you did overcome. And you will do it again.

- The only person stopping you from doing something is you. Keep believing in yourself, keep working hard, and it will happen.

- Try to stay positive by surrounding yourself with positivity, like friends who support you. Ignore those who are negative and try to bring you down – you don't need 'friends' like that.

- Have a purpose. Don't let the days pass you by – have some goals and targets, it doesn't matter how small they are. Whether it's doing 20 minutes of exercise every day, learning a new language or simply being able to finally French-plait your hair, you can do it!

- Send out good vibes! If you're a positive person to be around, people will want to hang out with you. Who wants to be around someone who always sees the worst in everything? And if you're being negative, all you will see around you is negativity.

- The best thing you can do is know yourself – are you sensitive? Stubborn? Nice? Mean? Work it out and then think about why you are the way you are. If you need to change, work on it, and if you don't, embrace who you are!

- Laugh it off – don't take life too seriously. Don't let one small thing ruin your day when you can just laugh about it later.

Lilly's Superheroes

In her vlogs, Lilly often talks about women who inspire her, and she has some pretty cool role models to choose from. It's no surprise that some of them, like Amy Schumer and Rebel Wilson, are stand-up comediennes and comic actresses since Lilly has shown her own skill at comedy; while it's easy to see why Lilly would love violinist/dancer/composer/writer Lindsey Stirling, since she is as multitalented as Lilly! Check out these impressive ladies who Lilly loves:

Amy Schumer

New Yorker Amy Schumer's comedy career started early – she was voted Class Clown (and also Teacher's Worst Nightmare!) when she graduated from school in 1999. After gaining a degree in theatre, she began performing stand-up comedy in 2004, and got her big break appearing on the US TV show *Last Comic Standing*. She appeared in the cult TV series *Girls* and *Curb Your Enthusiasm* and followed this with her own sketch show, *Inside Amy Schumer*. It was her first leading role in the movie Trainwreck (which she also wrote) that brought her worldwide fame, but her favourite job remains stand-up comedy, where she can talk about anything – and frequently does. Recently, she spoke up when *US Glamour* magazine described her as 'plus-sized' in a fashion feature, even though she is a US size 6 to 8 (UK 10 to 12). 'Young girls seeing my body type and thinking that is plus size? What are your thoughts? Mine are not cool, Glamour, not glamorous.'

Melissa McCarthy

You probably know that Melissa McCarthy is a hugely successful comic actress (*The Boss, Ghostbusters, Spy, The Heat, Bridesmaids*), but did you know she is also a stand-up comedienne and a fashion designer, too? Born in Illinois in 1970, she started performing comedy on stage before taking small roles in various movies including *Charlie's Angels*. In 2000, Melissa was cast as Sookie in the TV series *Gilmore Girls,* a role she played for seven years, and she followed this with the lead role of Molly in the sitcom *Mike & Molly*. It was her performance in *Bridesmaids* in 2011 that made her a megastar, however, and by 2015 she was rated the third highest-paid actress in Hollywood. Married with two children, Melissa also has her own clothing collection for plus-sized women called Seven7 which she launched because 'I've been every size on the planet and know that I didn't lose my sense of style just because I went above a size 12'.

Rebel Wilson

If you've seen *Bridesmaids* or *Pitch Perfect,* you'll know just how funny actress/comedienne Rebel can be. Born in Sydney, Australia, in 1980, she first became well known in her native Oz when she performed at the Melbourne Comedy Festival and then, in 2002, when she appeared in *The Westie Monologues* in Sydney which she wrote, starred in and produced. Over the next few years Rebel appeared on Australian TV comedy shows before moving to the US. It was there in 2011 that she won the role of Brynn in *Bridesmaids,* the mouthy sister to Matt Lucas's character (Rebel and Matt became such good friends they moved into a West Hollywood apartment together, which they shared for four years). Rebel has also hosted the MTV Movie Awards, acted in the movies *Grimsby, Pain & Gain, Night at the Museum: Secret of the Tomb, Pitch Perfect* and *Pitch Perfect 2* (as Fat Amy – a third movie is scheduled for 2017) and had her own comedy series, *Super Fun Night.*

Lindsey Stirling

California girl Lindsey was born in sunny Santa Ana in 1986 and began taking violin lessons when she was five. She had to choose between violin and dance lessons because her parents couldn't afford two sets of lessons. As she grew up, she realised she wanted to do both, and incorporated dance into her violin performances, which is a pretty tricky thing to do (you try playing a violin and dancing at the same time!). In 2010, Lindsey auditioned for the TV series *America's Got Talent* and reached the quarter-finals with her hip-hop violin style. She followed that with YouTube videos featuring her own original songs – you can watch her performances on her channel lindseystomp and her vlogs at LindseyTime – and she also collaborated with musicians including John Legend and Pentatonix. As well as winning numerous awards and having two bestselling albums, Lindsey has written an autobiography that she sent to Lilly (*The Only Pirate at the Party*) earlier this year.

#GirlLove Challenge

With over 6 million girls and women regularly watching Lilly's videos, Lilly realised that she had the perfect forum to tackle issues affecting women, especially one she hoped wouldn't exist for much longer – girl-on-girl hate.

So on 28 December 2015, Lilly launched the #GirlLove challenge with the help of friends Shay, Colleen, Gabbie, Andrea, Natalie, Brittany, Meg, Lindsey and many more. Noticing that girl-on-girl hate is a big thing at school, at work and online, where women and girls verbally attack each other and tear other girls down, Lilly suggested that we should do the opposite – celebrate other girls and women, applaud them, encourage each other and support each other. Here are some of the tips on how to do this from Lilly and her friends:

1. Look at other girls as sisters, not your competition.

2. We've all felt not good enough and not pretty enough, so we should all be able to relate to each other and support each other.

3. Don't put other girls down to make yourself feel better.

4. Girl-on-girl hate often stems from being jealous of another girl. Try not to be jealous, and instead admire that girl for all the things she has achieved.

5. Don't judge other girls or call them too fat or too skinny – try to find positive things to say instead.

6. You have the power to make another girl's day. Or you have the power to ruin it. Don't be that person who brings other people down.

7. Come up with a list of women you admire with your friends – it's much better to be positive and celebrate people than be negative. The women you admire can be friends, relatives, people in the public eye – the choice is yours!

Here's a table where you can write down your favourite five women, and why you admire them:

	Girl/Woman I Admire	Why I Admire Her
1		
2		
3		
4		
5		

8. Accept Lilly's challenge:

Post a tweet, Facebook status or Instagram post using the hashtag #GirlLove, complimenting or supporting another woman, and stop girl-on-girl hate today.

You can view Lilly's video at www.youtube.com/watch?v=ZQu3E0gU0ww and she will donate the money from the video's views to the Malala Fund, a fund that helps girls around the world to complete their education. You can read more at www.malala.org.

Superwoman Motivation!

Got exams coming up? A work project that was due last week? Or are you just determined to finish reading *War and Peace*/watching every season of *Game of Thrones*/getting firm abs before the end of the summer? Lilly is great at motivating herself and other people, and here are some of her tips to get you off the sofa and ready to start:

- Make a plan and say it out loud. Have you got a million things to do and don't know where to start? List them and make a plan as to how you are going to do them all. Then say it out loud – talk to yourself to convince yourself you can do it all, and you will do it! Be stern with yourself and firmly say it out loud so you know what you have to do and in what order.

- Have two to-do lists. One list is the list of things you are going to do TODAY, and the other is longer-term goals. That way, you don't just have one list that looks completely impossible when you get up in the morning! TIP: Rather than cross something out on your list when you have done it, have a Post-it note or whiteboard marked 'DONE' at the top and write what you have just done on that. You'll feel much more positive at the end of the day when you look at the Done list and see all you have achieved. Well done you!

- Keep your friends for fun times, not work times. Your friends may be great to go to the movies with or eat pizza with, but they're probably not that great at motivating you. So if you have work that needs to be done, either work alone or be in a room with people that work harder than you. It'll make you feel guilty, which will make you work harder. True!

- Kill distractions. Your phone does not control you – you don't have to reply to that text, call, WhatsApp message or tweet. If you have lots of work to do, turn your phone off, or at least put it on silent. Help your brain focus, so make sure you've got the TV turned off too. You won't get that essay finished if you're watching back-to-back episodes of *Say Yes to the Dress*.

- Most importantly, remember: **you can do it!**

Home Town Hero

TORONTO

Lilly grew up near Toronto, in Canada, but now spends much of her time in Los Angeles, partly because lots of her fellow YouTubers live there. 'This city [Toronto] has been the greatest comfort zone for me. All my friends are here, all my family is here, and I've accomplished so much here, but I know that it's going to require me to leave to progress in my career and follow my dreams,' she revealed in one of her vlogs. With her parents still based in Canada, Lilly is lucky enough to have a home in two of the most fun cities in the world – but which one should you visit? Check out the best of Toronto and LA below before you book your trip!

VS LA

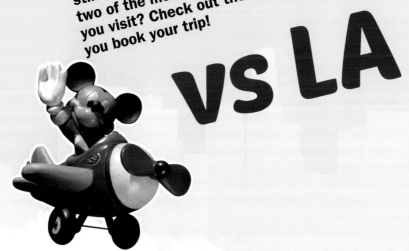

Toronto

'It might be one of the best cities in the world,' Lilly says of her former home town. She lived there with her mum, dad and sister in the Scarborough District. It's the most-populated city in Canada, home to over two and a half million people, and is known as one of the most cosmopolitan cities in the world. So what is there to see when you visit Toronto?

1. The CN Tower – one of the tallest buildings in the world. At 553.33m high (that's 147 floors), it was voted one of the seven wonders of the modern world by the American Society of Civil Engineers, along with the Empire State Building in New York, San Francisco's Golden Gate Bridge, the Panama Canal, the Channel Tunnel, the Itaipu Dam and the Delta Works in the Netherlands. Which is pretty impressive. There are various viewing platforms, and if you're really brave you could try the EdgeWalk, where you can walk on and around the roof while tethered to an overhead rail. Gulp.

2. Canada's Wonderland – this amusement park near Toronto is a must-visit for thrill fans. There is a water park, rides such as the Vortex, Shockwave, Behemoth and Leviathan – a roller coaster that runs at 148km/h.

3. Toronto Zoo – there are over 5,000 animals at the city's zoo, including gorillas, polar bears and two giant pandas on loan from China!

4. St Lawrence Market – feeling hungry? National Geographic called this open-air market the world's best food market. It's in the centre of historic Old Town Toronto, and some of the buildings date back to the early nineteenth century. This area, and the neighbouring Distillery Historic District, has lots of cool shops and restaurants, too.

5. Casa Loma – considered to be the only castle in Canada, this mansion looks like something from *Harry Potter* and is now a museum and has gardens you can walk around. Think it looks familiar? The house has been used as a location for movies including *X-Men*, *Chicago* and *Goosebumps*.

Toronto Weather

Perhaps the only downside to Toronto is its weather! It is very cold in the winter, with temperatures often dropping below freezing, and it is only really warm in the summer months when you might get temperatures reaching 26°C during June, July or August. So don't forget to pack a sweater!

LOS ANGELES

Lilly moved from Toronto to LA in December 2015. It was a scary move for her, leaving a place she loved, but she did gain a pretty apartment and continuous LA sunshine! Los Angeles is actually more than 80 neighbourhoods all merged together, including the beach town of Santa Monica, the Downtown business area, Hollywood, West Hollywood and Beverly Hills, so in one trip you'll only manage to see a small part of it. Never mind, you can always go back for more! Here are just a few highlights:

1. Disneyland – Actually in the area of Anaheim, south of LA, this is the original Disney theme park and now boasts two parks, Disneyland and Disney California Adventure. You'll find famous rides like Big Thunder Mountain Railroad, The Haunted Mansion, Indiana Jones Adventure, Pirates of the Caribbean, Star Tours and Radiator Springs Racers here, and a new Star Wars-themed land began construction in April 2016. Wait. We. Cannot.

2. Hollywood – Back in the 1950s and 1960s, Hollywood was the place to see and be seen. It's now very touristy and filled with people selling tacky souvenirs, but it's still worth passing through to see the stars' names cemented into the sidewalk on the Hollywood Walk of Fame, the footprints of famous actors and actresses outside the Chinese Theatre and the famous Hollywood sign in the distant mountains.

3. Santa Monica – There are lots of beach areas to the west of LA, including Venice with its infamous muscle beach where people go to show off their physique, and Malibu, home to many wealthy celebrities. The best town, however, is Santa Monica, with its amusement arcade on the pier, sandy beaches, fun shopping and dining area and, of course, lots of places to bask in the glorious sunshine.

4. Studios – Los Angeles is famous for all the movies that have been made here and there are still movie studios in the city. You can go on small tours of Warner Bros and sometimes catch the cast of *The Big Bang Theory* filming, as well as visit the preserved set of Central Perk Café from *Friends,* or visit Universal Studios, which is part working studio and part theme park. Rides there include a Jurassic Park water ride, a Despicable Me ride and the latest addition that opened in April 2016, the Wizarding World of Harry Potter.

5. Beverly Hills – If you have money – a LOT of money – you'll want to come to Beverly Hills to shop and dine. And if you don't have the money, it is still worth a visit so you can stride up Rodeo Drive and see all the designer stores and the limousines pulling up outside to collect all those shoppers who have just spent hundreds of thousands of dollars. Luckily it's not all aimed at those with trust funds and huge bank accounts – pop along to the shopping mall the Beverly Center for more regular shops such as famous American department stores Macy's and Bloomingdale's. Just don't spend all your dollars at once!

Los Angeles Weather

If you want sun, you've come to the right place. With an average temperature of 20°C in the winter and 28°C in the summer, LA is known for its sunny days, and there is very little rain, too. It's a pretty perfect climate; don't forget your suntan lotion and shades!

youtube
tips

Lilly has spent over six years posting YouTube videos, so we think she can be called an expert! Here are her tips about posting videos that are worth checking out before you start on your own YouTube career:

Don't make negative videos, and don't forward negative viral videos either. People are so desperate to make a video that goes viral that they are willing to capture someone's pain on camera to do so. And that isn't nice.

Make something that matters. If your YouTube clip is about a subject close to your heart, chances are there are other people who feel the same way and will like it too.

Spread the love! If you are thinking of making a video, how about doing one on something you love? Movies, fashion, games, your favourite chocolate spread, your friends – it's your choice! Let's share the things we want more of in this world.

Don't think making YouTube videos is sure to turn you into a millionaire. Contrary to rumours, YouTubers don't get paid per subscriber, for thumbs-ups/-downs or for comments. YouTubers get paid for the number of views the adverts before their videos get, and they get paid more if you click on those ads.

Speaking of ads, if you use material you don't have the copyright for – e.g. songs, movie clips, images – advertisers can't place ads on your videos. Sorry.

YouTubers also get paid for doing brand deals, where they mention and promote products in their videos. Brands only come calling when a YouTuber has millions of views though. So don't expect that deal with Coca-Cola just yet.

Making a video isn't as easy as it looks, so be sure you've got lots of time to spend on it. First, you have to film your video, often making something twice as long as the clip you'll end up posting on YouTube, as you will edit it down before you post it. As a rule of thumb, you will probably film two hours of footage just to get a 10-minute clip ready for YouTube!

Keep it short and sweet. Most YouTube videos are under 10 minutes long. Remember, lots of viewers follow loads of YouTubers, so you need to deliver something punchy and short to be added to the already long list of people they view regularly.

If you want to gain followers, you need to post regularly. For example, Lilly posts twice a week (usually Mondays and Thursdays), so her fans know when to expect a new video from her. If you only post occasionally, it's less likely you'll get people following you.

Be you. There are already lots of people doing every type of YouTube video you can think of, from make-up tutorials to comedy pranks to games walk-throughs. It's going to be hard to think of something completely new to video that no one has thought of, so instead, just make sure your version of something is unique to you. People watch Lilly because she is herself: funny, opinionated, interesting and unafraid to say what she thinks.

Try not to read any hateful comments! And if you do see them, try not to let them bother you. There really are people on the internet who have nothing better to do than write negative things for no reason. Don't change the way you are on YouTube just because someone has written something nasty in the comments.

Lilly's Best Sketches

Lilly is terrific at comedy, with fans especially loving the clips featuring her impersonations of her parents, and her chats to camera can also be really fun to watch, too. Here are just some of her best videos for you to check out:

'How Girls Get Ready'
more than 18 million views

Wondered why it takes so long for girls to get ready? In this comedy video, Lilly lifts the lid on her pre-evening routine as she tries on 20 outfits (19 of which she leaves on the floor), sings in the shower, watches a twerking video and burns herself while straightening her hair!

'Types of Kids at School'
more than 14 million views

One of Lilly's most popular videos, posted in 2012, this has Lilly ranting about the different types of kids at school. You'll recognise them all, from the Know-it-all, to the Hot Player, to Her Majesty – the girl who comes to school every day so dressed up you would think it was her wedding.

'#LEH'
more than 12 million views

This is the official video for Lilly and Humble's 2014 song '#LEH' – 'leh' is another word for 'ugh' or 'whatever' . . .

'How I Clean My Room'
more than 11 million views

Do you spend hours putting off cleaning your room? Check out this video of Lilly doing everything but tidy up!

'Types of Parents'
more than 10 million views

Lilly talks about the different types of parents (while her 'parents' are watching), including the cool cat parents who know everything about you and trust you, and the makeover failures – parents who try to change things, especially when they're comparing you to other people's kids.

'Nicki Minaj – "Anaconda": My Parents React'
more than 10 million views

Lilly has done lots of 'My Parents React' videos, and one of her fans' favourites is this one, in which she imagines her parents' reactions to Nicki Minaj's music video 'Anaconda'. 'It's going to be just like *The Jungle Book*,' says Lilly's dad! We don't think so . . .

'Types of Crushes'
more than 9 million views

In this video, Lilly chats about crushes, including her celebrity crush on The Rock, strangers that you fantasise about and the Never Mind crush, where you get to talk to your crush and discover you don't actually like them in person!

'How My Parents Fell In Love'
more than 8 million views

Kunal Nayyar co-stars in this video with Lilly, in which her 'parents' tell Lilly about how they met in June 1982 and married the following month. In a flashback, Kunal appears as the suave Raj, who was going to sweep Lilly's mother off her feet!

Lilly on Dating

It's hard to imagine Lilly has any time for dating, but when she does, she admits she often fails at it! Here are some of her dating conundrums . . .

Is it OK to Instagram during a date?

Lilly thinks probably not! And that means putting away Facebook, Snapchat and WhatsApp, too . . . if the only reason you're on this date is so you can Instagram it, maybe you are out with the wrong person?

Who should pay for the date?

While she's happy for the man to pay for the first date – he did ask her out, after all – Lilly thinks it should be fine if, further down the line, she gets to pay for an evening or two out, without the date being offended. Equal rights, ladies!

What do you wear on a date?

How do you pick an outfit that shows you're hot, but not trying so hard that you seem desperate! It's a tricky one, but the best advice is to wear something you feel comfortable in (so long as it's not trackpants and a hoodie – that's a little too casual!).

How do you know if you are exclusively dating someone?

If you're not sure whether he's seeing other people, remember, he's probably not sure whether you are either! The only way to sort this one out is to have that really awkward conversation and actually ask!

When should you make your new partner your entire world?

Ha! Trick question. The answer is, you shouldn't! Don't drop friends because you always want to spend time with your new love – they may not stick around waiting to pick up the pieces when he isn't around any more. Don't involve him/her in every single aspect of your life – your partner shouldn't be your 'other half' – you were a complete person before you met them!

Is it OK to fake who you are at the beginning of a new relationship?

While it's fine to be on your best behaviour for that all-important first date – maye not ordering the family-sized pizza for one and smother-ing it in ketchup, you know what we mean – don't fake who you are all the time. You want this new person in your life to like YOU, not some fake version of you. And besides, keeping up those fake appearances will be very tiring!

We're dating, what should our Facebook status be?

Stop it, stop it now! Yes, you're dating, and yes, you're happy. But if you change your Facebook status to 'in a relationship' after three days, 'like' everything he/she posts and every single one of your Facebook photos has your new love in it . . . take a step back. You are this close to having a relationship that's defined by social media, a place that's better suited to cute cat videos.

Super Rants

Sometimes things can just make you really, really mad, and Lilly gets as angry as the rest of us – and shares her often hilarious fury on YouTube! Here are just some of the things that drive her crazy:

Airlines

Lilly has ranted about flying – it's uncomfortable, she can't sleep, there are crying babies. But her 'What I Do On Airplanes' video shows that you wouldn't particularly want Lilly sat next to you on a flight either – after drinking gallons of water, it seems that she spends most of the flight getting up to use the toilet! And when she is not there, she's pressing the call button, squirming about in her seat or dribbling on the person sitting next to her.

People at Drive Thrus

Lilly admits that she goes to drive-thru takeaway restaurants a lot, even though it bugs her. She's either stuck behind someone going into far too much detail about their order ('can I have the burger but with no bun, ketchup on the side, make sure there are at least 50 fries with it...') who then checks it all before they drive off, people who pay for their order with change that they accidentally drop out of their car window, or those people who get to the drive-thru window and don't know what they want to eat. Arrrgghh!

Periods

Lilly has ranted about periods in two of her most-watched YouTube videos – they're really funny and worth checking out. Whether she's comparing period pains to having the spiky *Game of Thrones* throne sat on her ovary, talking about her hormones or telling boys about the ugly underwear girls wear during their periods, you can tell it's a subject that makes her brain explode!

Emojis

Think you know what emojis mean? In her video, Lilly calls out all the people who use fun emojis on their texts and WhatsApp messages to hide the fact that they are actually fuming, and reveals what people really mean when they send some of the little yellow characters such as the blushing emoji, the winky face and, of course, the pile of c**p one (Lilly says that one is reserved for texts to a certain airline – we think you can guess which one).

Her relationship status

Lilly googled herself and laughed about the results – there were lots of searches based on what she earns, whether she's married, gay, smokes or has a boyfriend! She even looked at some of the comments where people had written negative things about her, and did the right thing by shrugging it off. After all, she has millions of fans who love her!

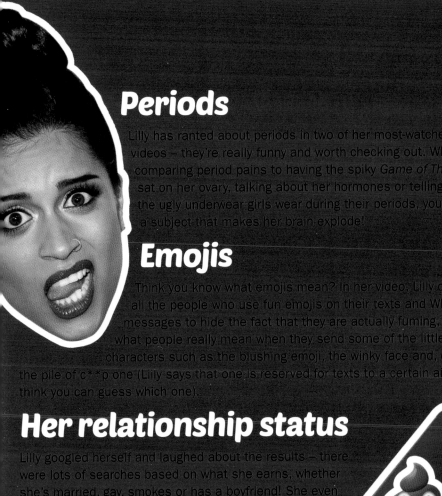

The Ultimate SUPERWOMAN QUIZ

So you think you know everything there is to know about Lilly Singh? Take the quiz below and find out just how much you really know about our favourite inspirational vlogger . . .

Answers on p.64

1. How much older than Lilly is Lilly's sister Tina?

a) four years

b) five years

c) six years

d) seven years

2. When Lilly was a baby, her sister Tina had an accident while she was holding Lilly. What happened?

a) she fell backwards onto a glass table, which broke

b) she tripped up the stairs and smashed her nose

c) she knocked over a saucepan of boiling water onto her feet

d) she dropped Lilly into the bath

3. If Lilly's house was on fire, what is the one item (not person) she would want to go back and get?

a) her TV

b) her sneakers

c) her clothes

d) her electronics – especially her laptop and phone

4. What is Lilly's favourite movie?

a) *White Chicks*

b) *Pretty Woman*

c) *Legally Blonde*

d) *The Notebook*

5. What is Lilly's favourite TV show?

a) *The Simpsons*

b) *The Good Wife*

c) *Dancing with the Stars*

d) *Game of Thrones*

6. Who is the one celebrity Lilly always wanted to meet?

a) Mark Wahlberg

b) Dwayne Johnson aka The Rock

c) Katy Perry

d) Matt Damon

What is Lilly's favourite restaurant?

a) TGI Fridays

b) McDonald's

c) Chipotle

d) Pizza Hut

How long did Lilly's dad give her to make a career out of YouTube before he'd ask her to go back to college to study for her master's?

a) six months

b) two years

c) five years

d) one year

Which city was the very first night of Lilly's tour?

a) Mumbai

b) Bangalore

c) Toronto

d) New Delhi

Do you know the area of LA where Lilly has an apartment? Is it:

a) Miracle Mile

b) Rodeo Drive

c) Santa Monica

d) West Hollywood

Lilly and Humble released a song in 2015 called '#IVIVI' – what does that stand for?

a) it's 416, the area code for Los Angeles

b) it's 441, the house number of Lilly's family home

c) it's 416, the area code for Toronto

d) it's 441, the area code for Toronto

Lilly has provided a voice for a 2016 animated movie. Does she appear in . . . ?

a) *Angry Birds*

b) *Ice Age: Collision Course*

c) *The Secret Life of Pets*

d) *Finding Dory*

Lilly got the name Superwoman from a piece of jewellery. What is it?

a) an S-shaped necklace

b) a Superwoman bracelet

c) a Superwoman pair of earrings

d) an S-shaped ring

In October 2015, Lilly made a twenty-first-century update of a very famous music video from the 1980s. Her version has had over two and a half million views, but what is it of?

a) George Michael's 'Careless Whisper'

b) Olivia Newton-John's 'Physical'

c) Whitney Houston's 'I Wanna Dance With Somebody'

d) Michael Jackson's 'Thriller'

In January 2016, Lilly appeared on *The Tonight Show Starring Jimmy Fallon* and he challenged her to play a quiz game. What was it?

a) Family Feud

b) Who Wants To Be A Millionaire?

c) The Price Is Right

d) Wheel Of Fortune

The Fu

So, what's next for multitalented Lilly Singh? Her sold-out world tour in 2015 showed that she was much, much more than just a YouTube vlogger – she's a comedienne, singer, rapper and actress – and someone who inspires millions of people around the world.

Lilly started 2016 with appearances on chat shows in the US that were a huge hit, so there are sure to be more TV appearances for her in the future, as well as opportunities for her to perform her own unique brand of comedy and music. Of course, the most important thing to her are her fans and her Superwoman channel – especially now that she has over eight million subscribers – so Lilly won't be leaving YouTube anytime soon.

We're not sure how the all-round star will fit everything in, but we're sure that whatever Lilly decides to do, it will be interesting, exciting and something we'll all definitely want to see!

ture...

?

ANSWERS

True or False

1. True;
2. False (sort of) – she was allergic when she was young but isn't anymore;
3. False, she doesn't swear at all . . . in English!;
4. True;
5. False – it was Baby Spice!;
6. True;
7. True;
8. False – she was a tomboy and hated wearing dresses;
9. True;
10. True;
11. False – it was *The Simpsons*;
12. True;
13. False, she hates bras;
14. False, it just got 70 views;
15. True;
16. False, she takes at least 60!
17. True;
18. True – sort of. The movie is actually a romantic comedy;
19. False, it's Kunal Nayyar, who plays Raj;
20. True.

Super Wordsearch

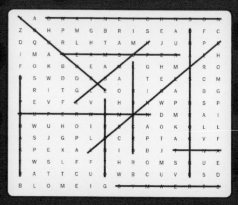

Ultimate Superwoman Quiz

1. c
2. a
3. d
4. a
5. d (though *The Simpsons* was her favourite growing up)
6. b
7. c
8. d
9. a
10. a
11. c
12. b
13. d
14. d
15. a